AF228451

ROMANS

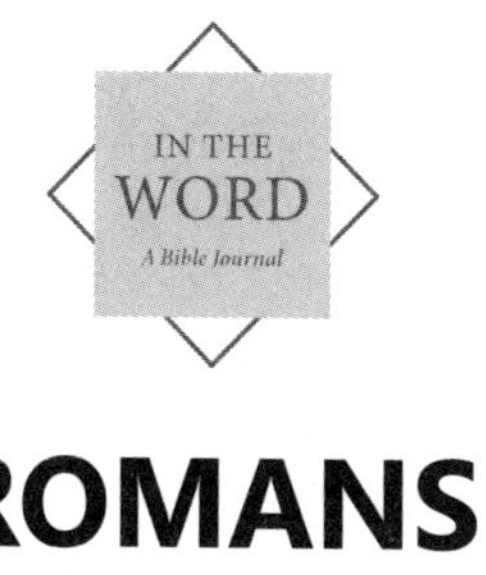

ROMANS

Rob Wynalda, Joel R. Beeke,
and Paul M. Smalley

REFORMATION HERITAGE BOOKS

Grand Rapids, Michigan

Romans
© 2025 by Reformation Heritage Books

Reformation Heritage Books
3070 29th St. SE
Grand Rapids, MI 49512
616-977-0889
orders@heritagebooks.org
www.heritagebooks.org

25 26 27 28 29 30/11 10 9 8 7 6 5 4 3 2

ISBN 979-8-88686-168-6

PREFACE

In Deuteronomy 17, Moses leaves final instructions concerning the future of Israel. As a prophet of God, he foretells that Israel will set a king over the nation (v. 14). This king must be an Israelite, not a foreigner (v. 15), and is forbidden to do certain things (vv. 16–17). In verse 18, Moses transitions to what the king should do. The king is commanded not to simply acquire a copy of the law (the entire book of Deuteronomy), but to handwrite his own copy of the law. The purpose was so that he would read it, fear the Lord, obey, avoid pride, not deviate, and enjoy a long reign (vv. 19–20; cf. Prov. 4:20–27).

More than three thousand years later, modern educators have discovered that students who write out notes by hand have a much higher retention rate than those who simply hear or visually read the information. Apparently, God knew this to be true for the kings of Israel also.

This series of books, known as The Bible Journal, was born from the insight found in Deuteronomy 17:18. Your Bible Journal gives you the opportunity to write out your own copy of a portion of the Holy Scriptures, just as the ancient kings of Israel were instructed to do. Writing out the words of the Bible helps a person to engage the Word of God by slowing down the process of reading the text. Writing answers to the discussion questions also helps you to thoughtfully engage the text. Furthermore, by completing a journal, you leave a legacy to pass on to future generations your insights and personal applications of the text (Deut. 6:6–9; Ps. 78:4–7).

To prepare you to meditate on this portion of the Holy Scriptures, we include an introduction to the book of the Bible to help you understand more thoroughly the Bible book you are about to write out in full. Study Questions and Devotional Reflections have been added after the blank pages set aside for copying each chapter of God's Word. The Study Questions focus on individual verses to keep you thinking about what you are writing, and the Devotional Reflections are designed to help you focus on a few of the major takeaways for your practical Christian life that each Bible chapter provides. We wish to thank Reformation Heritage Books for allowing us to use material drawn from *The Reformation Heritage KJV Study Bible* for the Bible Introduction material and for the Devotional Reflections. The Study Questions have been written by the authors of *The Bible Journal*. Thus, The Bible Journal walks you through a process of getting acquainted with a book of the Bible, copying a chapter by hand, reflecting on the meaning and application of that chapter, and then repeating the process for the next chapter. Families, friends, and small groups can work through a journal together, discussing their meditations for mutual edification as guided by the discussion questions.

The mass production of the Bible since the invention of the printing press has greatly blessed the world. However, there is also great benefit for Bible readers of all ages in following the Deuteronomy 17:18 principle and producing your own handwritten copy of the text.

May God richly bless you in writing and learning His Word through The Bible Journal (Rom. 1:16).

—Rob Wynalda, Joel R. Beeke, and Paul M. Smalley

Introduction to the Book of
ROMANS

AUTHORSHIP: The epistle was written by Paul, the apostle (1:1).

DATE: The apostle Paul appears to have written this letter from Corinth or its vicinity. This can be deduced from the references to Cenchrea (16:1), which was the port of Corinth, and to Gaius (16:23), who is also mentioned as a member of the Corinthian Church (1 Cor. 1:14). The reference to Erastus (also in Rom. 16:23) is consistent with the Corinthian connection in 2 Timothy 4:20. Paul stayed in Greece (probably largely in Corinth) for three months (Acts 20:2–3) on his way to Jerusalem with the collection from the Gentile churches for the poor saints there. Paul viewed this gift as extremely important, not only because the Jerusalem Christians had need of it but also because of its immense significance in cementing the unity between the Jewish and Gentile segments of the church. He makes reference to it in this epistle (Rom. 15:23–28). This would place the probable date of the writing of the epistle to the Romans at approximately AD 57 or 58.

THEME: Salvation by grace alone, especially justification by faith alone and the imputation of the righteousness of Jesus Christ to all who believe.

PURPOSE: To ground the believer's faith upon God's righteousness imputed through Christ alone, for the glory of God alone and for the unity of the church.

SYNOPSIS

The Contribution of Romans to Redemptive Revelation
The letter declares the apostle's intention to visit Rome and provides in advance a systematic treatment (1:1–8:39) of the gospel that he preaches and has been "separated unto" (1:1) as an apostle to the Gentiles. It stresses the unity of Jew and Gentile through this one gospel given by God to both (1:16; 3:9, 29–30; 4:16; 10:19–21; 11:30–31; 15:6; etc.). The letter also gives practical direction as to the proper fruit of

faith in Christ in various aspects of the Christian life (12:1–15:21). In God's goodness we have been given in this epistle the most systematic and extended demonstration of the true doctrine of the gospel anywhere in the inerrant Word of God. It is not surprising that God has used this part of His Word when bringing about rediscovery of the true gospel in history, particularly at the time of the Reformation.

The Church at Rome
We have no solid evidence of what means God had used to bring the church at Rome into existence. There is no reason to think that the apostle Peter had been to Rome prior to this time. Perhaps the most plausible explanation is that converts from Pentecost had gone to Rome. Other Christians may have immigrated from elsewhere and joined themselves to this church at the heart of the Empire. Without doubt there was a constant stream of travelers to and from Rome.

It becomes clear that there were both Jews and Gentiles in this church. The apostle addresses both directly (2:17; 11:13); he refers to his "kinsmen" (16:7, 11) yet magnifies his office as an apostle to the Gentiles and to the church and his intention to visit (1:5, 13). He was acquainted with some of its members (16:3–15, suggesting that the membership of the Roman church was predominantly Gentile.

The Use of the Word "Justification" in Romans
It is of great importance in understanding this majestic epistle that we get a clear grasp of what the term "justification" means in its usage by the apostle Paul. We can say the following:

1. Justification is an act of God. "It is God that justifieth" (8:33). God is the ultimate Judge, beyond whom there is no appeal.

2. Justification is God declaring guilty sinners righteous. He "justifieth the ungodly" (4:5). "Justification" is used as a legal term and is the opposite of condemnation (8:34).

3. God does not justify all the ungodly. He is "just, and the justifier of him which believeth in Jesus" (3:26).

4. God justifies believing sinners by imputing to them ("crediting to" or "reckoning to" their account) the righteousness of Jesus Christ (4:25; 8:34). This includes Christ's righteousness

in both His passive obedience (suffering the wrath of God in the place of sinners) and His active obedience (keeping God's law on their behalf). It is this righteousness of Christ that is referred to by the phrase "righteousness of God" (1:17; 3:22; 10:3), as revealed in the gospel.

5. Faith is not an alternative righteousness but the sole instrument of justification. God justifies believing sinners, "not by imputing faith itself, the act of believing, or any other evangelical obedience, to them as their righteousness; but by imputing the obedience and satisfaction of Christ unto them, they receiving and resting on him and his righteousness by faith; which faith they have not of themselves; it is the gift of God" (Westminster Confession of Faith, 11.1).

Justification and Sanctification
Keeping a clear distinction between these two biblical terms is important to understanding the book of Romans and the biblical gospel. Justification relates to God declaring the sinner righteous. It refers to a legal standing, the removal of the guilt of sin and the constituting of the sinner as righteous before God. Justification is available to believers on account of Christ's imputed righteousness.

Sanctification relates not to being *declared* righteous but to being made righteous. It means being separated to God or being made holy. It addresses not the guilt of sin but the actual presence, pollution, and practice of sin. It has in view an imparted, as opposed to an imputed, righteousness in Christ.

This distinction explains why, for example, the Westminster Shorter Catechism (Q. 33 and 35) speaks of justification as an "act of God" and sanctification as a "work of God." Justification is something God declares about His people, whereas sanctification is something He does to His people. Chapter 6 of Romans shows that the justified man is invariably a changed man. He has been and is continuously being sanctified. Nevertheless, though both these blessings (justification and sanctification) are bestowed by Christ upon His people (and never only one without the other), they are two different gifts, and the distinction between them must not be blurred. Holiness of life is the evidence of true faith in Christ, but it is by faith alone, through the imputation of Christ's merits alone, that we are justified (3:21, 28; 4:6; etc.).

Roman Catholicism historically has failed to distinguish between justification and sanctification. Although the Roman Catholic Church asserts that Christ's righteousness merits our justification, nevertheless it pronounces a curse on anyone who claims that Christ's righteousness is actually declared to be ours. In this view justification is both the forgiveness of sins and the renewal of the soul. Thus justification is by means of the sanctifying process in this life and continued in the next as necessary. This is contrary to the biblical doctrine of justification so clearly presented in Paul's epistle to the Romans.

The stand taken by Martin Luther by the grace of God in the Protestant Reformation of the sixteenth century has not become redundant. The Lord who spoke by the prophets and in these last days by His Son (Heb. 1:1–2) has also given us apostolic epistles to expound the meaning of Christ's redeeming work and to elucidate the doctrine of salvation. The epistle to the Romans is central to that culmination of God's revelation to men.

OUTLINE

I. Introduction (1:1–17)
   A. Greeting (1:1–7)
   B. Declaration of Resolve to Visit (1:8–15)
   C. Summary of the Gospel That Paul Preaches (1:16–17)

II. The Doctrine of the Gospel (1:18–8:39)
   A. Gospel Basics (1:18–3:31)
      1. The Gentiles Are Sinners (1:18–32)
      2. The Jews Are Sinners (2:1–3:8)
      3. All Have Sinned (3:9–20)
      4. The Only Hope Is God's Righteousness Provided in Christ (3:21–31)

   B. Old Testament Confirmation (4:1–25)
      1. Abraham and Justification (4:1–5)
      2. David and Justification (4:6–8)
      3. Justification Independent of Circumcision (4:9–12)
      4. Promise and Law (4:13–17)
      5. Abraham's Faith to Be Followed (4:18–25)

   C. The Blessedness and Safety of the Justified (5:1–11)
   D. Justification in Christ as Sure as Condemnation in Adam (5:12–21)
   E. The Forgiven Man Is Being Made Holy (6:1–23)

Notes

1

2

3

4

5

6

7

8

Notes

9

10

11

12

13

14

15

Notes

16

17

18

19

20

21

Notes

22

23

24

25

26

27

Notes

28

29

30

31

32

STUDY QUESTIONS

1. Verses 1–2: What does Paul say about the gospel?

2. Verses 3–4: What does Paul say about Jesus (the message of the gospel)?

3. Verse 7: How does Paul describe believers?

4. Verse 8: Whom does Paul thank for their faith? Why?

5. Verses 11–12: What are Paul's goals in coming to the church in Rome?

6. Verse 16: Why is Paul not ashamed of the gospel?

7. Verse 18: What is God revealing from heaven? How should knowing that affect us?

8. Verse 20: How do people know that there is a God?

9. Verse 24: What has God done to those who worship creatures instead of the Creator?

10. Verses 26–27: What does this teach about homosexuality?

11. Verse 32: How does this verse show that sinners have no excuse?

DEVOTIONAL REFLECTIONS

1. All true ministers of Christ are separated unto the gospel (v. 1), and the church must devote itself to the preaching of the good news. Do not be ashamed of the gospel (v. 16) nor of its doctrinal content (6:17). There is no gospel without the announcement of God's gift of righteousness through faith in Jesus Christ (1:17) and the realities of sin and God's wrath (v. 18; 1 John 4:10). The church must declare both His love and justice.

2. If men do not love God, they will not love their neighbors (v. 18). Ungodliness and unrighteousness go together. Those who give away God in exchange for idols will find that God gives them over to many sins, including homosexual lusts and practices. When God gives a people over to sin (Rom. 1:24, 26, 28), it is as though they are blinded at noonday. How is that spiritual and moral blindness evident in the world around you today?

3. Before Paul explains in detail the good news of salvation, he details the guilt and misery of sin. Why must we know God's justice and wrath against sin if we are ever to know the saving mercy of Jesus Christ? How does this gospel of justice against sin and grace to sinners promote true gratitude and enduring love for God?

Notes

1

2

3

4

5

6

Notes

7

8

9

10

11
12

13

Notes

14

15

16

17

18

19

20

Notes

21

22

23

24

25

26

Notes

27

28

29

STUDY QUESTIONS

1. Verses 1–3: What does Paul say about people who are judgmental toward others?

2. Verses 4–5: How should God's goodness affect people? What if they do not respond rightly?

3. Verses 8–9: What will happen to those who do evil?

4. Verse 12: What will happen to Gentiles "without law"—that is, without the Bible?

5. Verse 15: How do even the Gentiles have some knowledge of right and wrong?

6. Verse 20: What did the Jews have in the law?

7. Verse 24: What was the result of the Jews' hypocrisy in not keeping their own law?

8. Verses 28–29: Who is the true Jew, even if uncircumcised? Is this true of you?

DEVOTIONAL REFLECTIONS

1. The unbelieving Jews convinced themselves that they were not really sinners in God's sight by comparing themselves to Gentiles. Do you try to evade the reality of your guilt before God by comparing yourself with others rather than by assessing yourself against the standard of God's law? Why does this kind of comparison fail to excuse our sins?

2. Those who do not hear the gospel are still condemned as guilty sinners (v. 12). Otherwise, the preaching of the gospel would be best avoided, as exposure to it would risk making innocent people guilty. The evangelistic imperative rests on the fact that all who are without Christ are lost, and "how shall they believe in him of whom they have not heard?" (10:14). How should this motivate Christians to spread the gospel?

3. The Lord will judge the "secrets of men" (Rom. 2:16), even what is hidden from those closest to us. Having a Bible and knowing its contents, while good, is not enough (vv. 17–18). People may think highly of us and praise our devotion to God, but that devotion is meaningless unless God sees evidence of His saving work in our hearts (v. 29; see John 5:44). How should these truths drive us to seek Christ?

1

2

3

4

5

6

7

Notes

8

9

10

11

12

13

14

15
16

17

18

Notes

19

20

21

22

23

24

Notes

25

26

27

28

29

Notes

30

31

STUDY QUESTIONS

1. Verses 1–2: What was the chief advantage of belonging to the circumcised people of God?

2. Verse 4: What Scripture passage does Paul quote? What does it mean in its context?

3. Verse 9: What is true of both Jews and Gentiles?

4. Verses 10–12: What is man's state apart from God's saving grace?

5. Verse 18: What is lacking in sinful mankind? How can we see that in the ways people act?

6. Verses 19–20: What is one purpose of the law? What is the law unable to do for sinners?

7. Verses 24–25: How can sinners be justified—that is, declared righteous by God? Look up the words "redemption" and "propitiation." What do they mean?

8. Verse 26: How can God be just and the justifier of sinners who believe in Jesus?

9. Verse 28: What do works of obedience to the law add to a sinner's justification?

10. Verse 31: Does the gospel nullify the law? Why or why not?

1. No amount of human consensus can overturn the truth of God (v. 4). The final appeal for Christians is not any national court or international convention, nor the court of public opinion, but the Word of God. Also, the false conclusions of others do not justify rejection of the truth (v. 5). The truth of the Bible must be believed. Sinners will always want a gospel that allows them to continue in sin (v. 8), but the apostle Paul draws out the unbeliever from every false refuge, whether trust in a name or ordinances (v. 1), or in false reasoning (vv. 5–8). Have you given up all your excuses and arguments and submitted to God's Word as your ultimate authority?

2. Christ is the object of our faith; our own believing cannot be. We must look outside ourselves to Christ (v. 22). The Old Testament testifies that we must look to Christ (v. 21). Our only hope of righteousness is not in our works of obeying God's law (v. 20) but in Christ's work of redeeming sinners at the cost of His precious blood (vv. 24–25). Christ alone can satisfy God's justice directed against sinners and appease His righteous wrath against those who dishonor Him (vv. 25–26). Anyone, Jew or Gentile, who trusts in Christ alone is declared righteous by the supreme Judge (vv. 22, 30). Thus the Lord says to all who hear the gospel, "Behold me, behold me" (Isa. 65:1). Have you cast aside your self-righteousness and received and rested upon Christ as your only righteousness before God?

Notes

1

2

3

4

5

6

7

8

Notes

9

10

11

12

13

Notes

14

15

16

17

18

Notes

19

20

21

22

23

24

25

STUDY QUESTIONS

1. Verses 2–3: How was Abraham justified?

2. Verses 4–5: What is the difference between justification by works and justification by grace?

3. Verse 10: When was Abraham reckoned righteous by God? Why is that important?

4. Verses 11–12: Who are Abraham's spiritual children?

5. Verse 15: What does the law result in for sinners? Please explain.

6. Verses 17–21: What does this passage teach us about faith? How have you exercised faith?

7. Verses 22–25: What does God promise to those who trust in Christ crucified and raised from the dead?

DEVOTIONAL REFLECTIONS

1. Abraham believed the gospel (John 8:56; Gal. 3:8, 17), as did Moses (Heb. 11:24–26) and David (Ps. 32). There has only been one way of salvation for any sinner since the fall of man in the garden of Eden (Gen. 3:15), and there will be only this one way until the end of the world (Rev. 22:17). Only in Christ is there acceptance with God. We must trust in the one Seed, Jesus Christ, in whom many of Abraham's literal seed and sinners from all nations are blessed (Gal. 3:16).

2. Even the greatness of your sins does not exclude you from the promise of mercy. God justifies the ungodly (Rom. 4:5) who trust in Christ. You must not "stagger" at the promise of God. Do not say "I do not know whom to believe" because you should know. You must believe God (2 Tim. 1:12). Take your great sins to God and seek forgiveness in Christ. Tell Him your great need, as David did: "For thy name's sake, O LORD, pardon mine iniquity; for it is great" (Ps. 25:11). He has purposed to make Himself known as the God of grace (Rom. 9:23; Eph. 3:9–10). Why do sinners sometimes shrink back from trusting Christ? How can this chapter encourage them to come without delay?

3. Believing glorifies God (Rom. 4:20) by acknowledging His power and truthfulness: He can and will perform what He has promised in accordance with His love for His people and His justice in accepting them for Christ's sake. Honor God by trusting Him.

Notes

1

2

3

4

5

6

7

Notes

8

9

10

11

12

13

Notes

14

15

16

17

Notes

18

19

20

21

STUDY QUESTIONS

1. Verse 1: How does justification by faith change our relationship with God?

2. Verse 3: How can understanding justification by faith change our attitude toward troubles?

3. Verses 6–8: How did God demonstrate the greatness of His love? How does this affect you?

4. Verse 12: How did sin and death enter the world?

5. Verses 15–17: How does Paul contrast Adam and Christ?

6. Verse 19: What did Christ do to make His people righteous?

7. Verse 21: What are the two reigns or kingdoms in this present world?

1. Do you have peace with God (v. 1)? This is not a question of your feelings but of your objective standing before God. Only when you have been forgiven and declared righteous through faith in Christ can you experience "the peace of God, which passeth all understanding" (Phil. 4:7).

2. Glorying in tribulations is no easy thing, even for a strong believer. We must take to heart the truth of God's providential government over all of our circumstances and trust His wisdom, power, and promised grace, which ensure that all things work for our good. Only then will we be able to accept that those things that seem to harm us are actually still sent for our good (2 Cor. 12:7–10). We must also rest our hearts upon the righteousness of God in Christ. Why is a sense of peace with God necessary in order for us to glory in trials?

3. Christianity is not just a set of principles for living but a claim about history. This chapter presupposes that Adam was a literal and historical individual. Genesis 1:1–3:24 must be understood that way if we are to make sense of Romans 5. We see, also, the importance of the virgin birth. Christ was not, in His human nature, descended from Adam by ordinary generation, and so the guilt of Adam's first transgression was not imputed to Him under the covenant of works. This means that, as the perfectly guiltless Mediator of the covenant of grace, He can act as the substitute for His people (2 Cor. 5:21). Why do the faith and hope of Christians stand or fall on the historical reality of these two persons, Adam and Christ?

Notes

1

2

3

4

5

6

7

Notes

8

9

10

11

12

13

14

Notes

15

16

17

18

19

Notes

20

21

22

23

STUDY QUESTIONS

1. Verses 1–2: Why can't believers live in sin anymore?

2. Verse 6: How was the ruling power of sin destroyed for Christ's people?

3. Verse 11: How should believers view themselves in light of Christ's work?

4. Verses 12–13: What responsibility do believers have?

5. Verses 17–18: Why is Paul thanking God? What is he teaching about salvation?

6. Verse 21: What is the believer's attitude to his or her past sins? Is this your experience?

7. Verse 22: What is the path to eternal life? Are you on that path?

8. Verse 23: What is the contrast here between "wages" and "gift"?

DEVOTIONAL REFLECTIONS

1. People often love to talk about the privileges of God's children, but they may neglect to realize that union with Christ means that we have died and risen with Him. This must show itself in our lives. Though justification is entirely through faith, true faith brings the effects of Christ's cross into our lives to crucify the old self. How then can believers continue comfortably in sin? His resurrection overflows by the Spirit into each of those for whom He died and brings to life a person who loves God. How then can believers fail to live for Him? How is a person who claims to be one with Christ and yet lives for sin and is dead toward God a stark contradiction?

2. We all serve someone (v. 16). If it is the world, the flesh, and the devil, the idea that this is true freedom is an illusion. Sinners are in fact slaves of their own thoughts and desires (Titus 3:3). However, salvation in Christ does not set us free to live for ourselves, for this is the very slavery we must escape. When God joins a sinner to Christ, that sinner becomes a willing slave of Christ to do His righteous will. Serving Christ is true freedom (John 8:36). Why is this so? Are you a slave of Christ?

Notes

Chapter 7

1

2

3

4

Notes

5

6

7

8

9

10

11

12

13

14

15

Notes

16

17

18

19

20

21

22

23

Notes

24

25

STUDY QUESTIONS

1. Verses 1–2: How does Paul illustrate that only death releases us from the law?

2. Verse 4: How did Christ release His people from the law so that they could be His?

3. Verses 5–6: What is the difference between these two spiritual states?

4. Verses 7–8: How does sin react to God's law?

5. Verse 12: What does Paul say about the law?

6. Verse 15: What greatly frustrates Paul? How have you experienced the same frustration?

7. Verse 20: What is the cause of the believer's continuing spiritual frustration?

8. Verse 22: What indication is there in this verse that Paul describes a believer?

DEVOTIONAL REFLECTIONS

1. The law reveals to us our sin and therefore our need for Christ, the Savior of sinners (v. 7; Mark 10:17–21; John 4:16–18; Acts 2:36–37). Conviction of sin alone is not conversion to Christ. The holy law can be like sunshine on a stagnant pond that makes it stink even worse than before (Rom. 7:8–13). Felix trembled but was not converted (Acts 24:25). Nevertheless, there can be no trusting in Christ to save us if we are oblivious to the sin from which we must be saved. How has God's law uncovered your sin? How has it helped you to see your need for Christ?

2. If we are in Christ, the battle is not over but the victory is sure (Rom. 7:25). He has purchased our sanctification and glorification, as well as our justification (8:1–39). However, we cannot ignore the experiential struggle in the Christian's soul between what is ideal and what is actual. Godly believers are often deeply frustrated over their lack of conformity to God's holy commands. While they need to be encouraged to press on in the battle, they also need to be comforted with the truth that this is the normal experience of believers on earth. How might losing sight of this truth lead to deep discouragement? How might it lead to hypocrisy and superficiality in the church?

Notes

1

2

3

4

5

6

Notes

7

8

9

10

11

12

Notes

13

14

15

16

17

18

Notes

19

20

21

22

23

24

25

Notes

26

27

28

29

30

Notes

31

32

33

34

35

36

Notes

37

38

39

STUDY QUESTIONS

1. Verses 1–2: How does Paul describe the spiritual state of those in Christ?

2. Verse 3: How did God do what the law could not accomplish?

3. Verses 7–8: What is the spiritual state of those outside of Christ?

4. Verse 9: What is true of everyone who belongs to Christ?

5. Verses 12–13: What must people do in order to avoid eternal death and gain eternal life?

6. Verses 14–16: How does the Holy Spirit minister within the children of God?

7. Verse 18: What does Paul say about our present sufferings and the coming glory?

8. Verse 21: What will creation receive when it is rescued from corruption and suffering?

9. Verses 26–27: What is another way that the Spirit helps believers?

10. Verse 28: What promise is given here? To whom does this promise belong?

11. Verses 29–30: What will God do for those whom He foreknew and predestined?

12. Verses 31–35: How does this show us what "more than conquerors" (v. 37) means?

13. Verse 36: How does this show us what "more than conquerors" (v. 37) does not mean?

14. Verses 38–39: What does this promise mean to you personally?

DEVOTIONAL REFLECTIONS

1. Knowing the law, on its own, will not eradicate the love for sin (v. 3). Walking in the Spirit, however, is not some mystical experience; rather, this occurs when the Spirit of God fills our hearts with loving gratitude to God for His love in Christ and we express that by fulfilling God's law (v. 4). As children of a good Father, believers realize that sin never does them any good (v. 13) but that the ways of God are life and peace (v. 6). All their lives are in His loving hands, and He will bring His adopted children to the glory of His Son (vv. 28–29). How do these truths motivate you to love and obey God?

2. To call God "Father" (v. 15) is an immense privilege. The divine love behind this word is breathtaking. God did not spare His only begotten Son but gave Him up so that sinners thereby might have God. God adopted His enemies as His children, and He gives them His Spirit to stir them to call Him Abba, or Father. Why are we so reluctant to draw near to Him? How can Romans 8 encourage us to be more faithful and fervent in prayer?

Notes

1

2

3

4

5

6

7

Notes

8

9

10

11

12

13

14

15

16

17

18

19

20

21

Notes

22

23

24

25

26

27

Notes

28

29

30

31

32

33

1. Verses 2–3: What does Paul feel because of Jews who have not believed in Christ?

2. Verse 6: Why doesn't Israel's rejection of Christ prove that God's word failed?

3. Verse 11: Why was one of Rebecca's children exalted above the other?

4. Verses 15–16: Why are some saved and others not? How is that humbling?

5. Verses 20–21: What is Paul's answer to those who object against predestination?

6. Verses 22–23: What are God's purposes for those to be damned and those to be saved?

7. Verses 25–29: What Scripture passages does Paul quote? Why?

8. Verse 32: Why did the Jews, who sought righteousness, not attain it?

1. The strength of Paul's expression of compassion for the lost (vv. 1–3) may startle us; it should. We are to love our neighbors as ourselves. If we care about not going to hell ourselves, how can we be indifferent to our neighbors being on the broad road that leads to destruction? How does this challenge you to pray and to take action?

2. God is absolutely sovereign over the will of men. Even sinful acts, though God does not condone them (nor is He the author of sin), are included in the plan of God (Gen. 50:20; 2 Sam. 16:9–11; 2 Chron. 18:20–22; Ps. 76:10). Even the fact that the holy angels did not fall is based on God's sovereign election (1 Tim. 5:21). We should believe the doctrine of God's sovereign predestination on the testimony of Holy Scripture (Rom. 9:12–13, 15, 17). It is not incompatible with evangelistic concern (vv. 1–3), however difficult it may seem to reconcile the two. How can trusting that God is in control give us confidence and freedom to faithfully proclaim the gospel?

3. We should not try to guess whom, among the unconverted, are God's elect. "Front-runners" can remain unregenerate, whereas "unpromising candidates" may come to faith in Christ (vv. 30–31). How should this encourage us to preach the gospel to all kinds of people?

Notes

1

2

3

4

5

6

7

Notes

8

9

10

11

12

13

14

Notes

15

16

17

18

19

Notes

20

21

STUDY QUESTIONS

1. Verse 1: How does Paul respond to the unbelief of Israel? How is he an example to us?

2. Verse 5: What does the law require for righteousness?

3. Verse 9: How can a person be saved?

4. Verses 14–15: Why must gospel preachers go and minister to all peoples?

5. Verse 17: How does God give saving faith to people?

6. Verse 21: What is God's posture, humanly speaking, toward Israel? What does this mean?

DEVOTIONAL REFLECTIONS

1. Paul's prayer (v. 1) indicates both his belief that salvation is in God's hands and his compassion toward the unbelieving. There is no contradiction here (Acts 26:29). Nor are there valid excuses for unbelief (Rom. 10:6–9). You have a Bible in your hand to read. It is your duty to believe. And there is within it every encouragement to trust Christ. He is rich (v. 12) to all who do believe, bestowing upon them such great mercies as forgiveness of sin, peace with God, and the hope of glory for all who do so (Ps. 86:5). How should this encourage evangelism? How should this impress upon all who hear the gospel their need to trust in Christ?

2. The preaching of the gospel is vital as the means appointed by the sovereign God for the ingathering of His elect (Rom. 10:13–15). We have no divine authorization from Scripture to believe that people dying without the knowledge of God's Word will be saved by some other means (Acts 4:12). Sinners must believe in Christ in order to be saved, and they must hear the gospel in order to believe. How should this motivate churches and seminaries to train and send out laborers to preach the gospel everywhere on earth? How can you help?

Notes

1

2

3

4

5

6

Notes

7

8

9

10

11

12

Notes

13

14

15

16

17

18

Notes

19

20

21

22

23

24

25

26

27

28

29

30

31

Notes

32

33

34

35

36

STUDY QUESTIONS

1. Verse 1: Has God completely rejected Israel? How do we know?

2. Verses 5–6: What does this teach us about election, grace, and works?

3. Verses 7–8: What did God do with those He had not chosen for salvation?

4. Verse 11: What was God's purpose in permitting Israel to stumble over Christ?

5. Verses 16–17: What does the tree represent? What is Paul teaching?

6. Verse 20: Why are some branches broken off? How do others stand?

7. Verses 25–26: What mystery is Paul revealing here?

8. Verse 29: What does Paul say about God? What does this imply about the Jews?

9. Verses 33–36: How would you write this doxology in your own words?

DEVOTIONAL REFLECTIONS

1. The apostle treats David's prayer for God's punishment on the wicked (Ps. 69:22–23) as the Word of God (Rom. 11:9–10) as surely as the prophecies of Christ's sufferings in that Psalm (Ps. 69:9, 20–21), and so should we. We should read and sing such psalms without embarrassment. If we have a problem with them, the problem lies in our minds and hearts, not in the Word of God.

2. The gospel has come to us in our various nations, but it was not always so (Acts 14:16). We should be thankful to God, for He did not owe us the gospel! When was the last time you thanked God that you have heard the good news? How can the last four verses of this chapter help you to worship God for His saving plans?

3. Though Christians debate God's future plans for the physical descendants of Abraham, Isaac, and Jacob (Rom. 11:25), we should all join Paul in praying for their conversion (10:1). Let us devote ourselves to praying "that the kingdom of sin and Satan may be destroyed, the gospel propagated throughout the world, the Jews called, the fullness of the Gentiles brought in...that Christ would rule in our hearts here, and hasten the time of his second coming, and our reigning with him forever" (Westminster Larger Catechism, A. 191). Do you pray for these things? If not, why not?

Notes

1

2

3

4

5

Notes

6

7

8

9

10

11

12

13

Notes

14

15

16

17

18

19

20

21

STUDY QUESTIONS

> 1. Verses 1–2: What should Christians do in response to God's mercies?
>
> 2. Verses 4–5: How does Paul describe the church?
>
> 3. Verse 9: What does this teach us about true love?
>
> 4. Verse 15: How would you explain what this commandment requires of us?
>
> 5. Verse 19: What can help Christians not take revenge?
>
> 6. Verse 20: What is the opposite of taking revenge?

DEVOTIONAL REFLECTIONS

1. When we have experienced something of the misery of our sin along with the deliverance given in Jesus Christ, our hearts will respond with the love of true gratitude. This is the practical fruit of the gospel: "What shall I render unto the LORD for all his benefits toward me?" (Ps. 116:12). Rather than yearning to fit in with the world, we are to devote the whole of our lives, mind and body, to learning and doing God's will. How can the Christian live as a priest, offering every day as a sacrifice to God?

2. Real love must express itself in service. For this cause God gave various spiritual gifts to empower His people to serve. However, rather than waiting with anxiety until we know what our gifts are, God calls us to give ourselves to the life of a servant of God, cheerfully and fervently caring for each other. How do you serve?

3. The key to combating vengefulness is to know our place before God. He is the Judge; we are not. When people wrong us, let us remember that it is not about our honor but about the glory of God. How can the Lord's statement "Vengeance is mine; I will repay" (Rom. 12:19) set us free from any impulse to take personal vengeance in word or deed?

Notes

1

2

3

4

5

Notes

6

7

8

9

10

11

Notes

12

13

14

STUDY QUESTIONS

1. Verse 1: What does Paul teach concerning civil authorities and our duty to them?

2. Verse 4: What does Paul call the civil ruler? What does "the sword" refer to?

3. Verse 8: What is our basic obligation to our neighbor according to God's law?

4. Verses 11–13: What does Paul mean by "sleep," "night" and "day," and "darkness" and "light"?

5. Verse 14: What does it mean to "put on" Christ (Gal. 3:27; Eph. 4:24; 6:11; Col. 3:10, 12; 1 Thess. 5:8)?

DEVOTIONAL REFLECTIONS

1. Our duty to civil authority should be determined by God-given biblical principle, not by the degree of our fear of getting caught in an infraction (Rom. 13:5). Though people around us may neither give honor to authority nor exercise authority in an honorable way, Christians must be people who conscientiously honor authority because they honor God. What would that have meant for Christians in pagan Rome? What about for you?

2. We need God's law to tell us how to love (vv. 8–10). There is no conflict between law and love. Love is a command, and the Ten Commandments show us in greater detail what that means. The Old Testament taught love, even to our enemies (Ex. 23:4–5). There is no difference in moral standards between the testaments, though the same standard is more fully revealed in the New Testament.

Notes

1

2

3

4

5

6

Notes

7

8

9

10

11

12

13

Notes

14

15

16

17

18

19

20

Notes

21

22

23

STUDY QUESTIONS

1. Verse 1: How should we treat believers who are weak in the faith?

2. Verse 4: Why is it wrong to judge another Christian, especially in morally indifferent things?

3. Verse 8: What is the great purpose that directs the lives of all true believers?

4. Verses 10–13: What doctrine can motivate us not to be judgmental? How does it do so?

5. Verse 17: What does Paul teach concerning God's kingdom?

6. Verse 19: What principles should guide us when we disagree with other Christians about matters that are not clearly commanded or forbidden in the Bible?

7. Verse 23: What is true about anything done without faith? Why is that so (Heb. 11:6)?

DEVOTIONAL REFLECTIONS

1. We should rebuke blatant sin and rebellion (Lev. 19:17) but exercise restraint and gentleness toward those young in the faith and those who need encouragement in the ways of the Lord, rather than condemning them for every defect arising from ignorance or a misguided conscience. This is not a compromising of holiness but an exercise of it, for the essence of holiness is love. What kinds of issues does the church face today where some are bound by conscience in matters not commanded in Scripture, while others are free? How should they bear with each other in mutual love and respect?

2. We should never disturb the peace of the church except over a matter of real and vital principle (Rom. 14:19). Rather than crusading for our own views in matters of minor importance, we should be zealous for peace. We should also seek greater illumination of our brothers' minds and consciences through prayer and the Word, for coercing people into conformity without real conviction is a hollow victory. In what ways does this principle require a great deal of patience toward other Christians?

Notes

Chapter 15

1

2

3

4

5

6

7

Notes

8

9

10

11

12

13

Notes

14

15

16

17

18

19

Notes

20

21

22

23

24

25

26

Notes

27

28

29

30

31

32

33

STUDY QUESTIONS

1. Verse 2: How should Christians treat each other?

2. Verses 5–6: What is one purpose of being united with other believers?

3. Verses 9–12: What Scripture passages does Paul quote here?

4. Verse 13: What do we learn about hope? Why is hope a desirable and beneficial grace?

5. Verse 16: How was Paul like an Old Testament priest?

6. Verses 20–21: What was Paul's priority in ministry? Who is like him today?

7. Verses 25–27: Why was Paul going to Jerusalem? Why was that good and right?

8. Verse 29: What did Paul expect would happen if he came to Rome?

9. Verse 32: Why might Paul have added "by the will of God"?

DEVOTIONAL REFLECTIONS

1. The attitude that says "It's my life; I'll please myself" is ungodly and inconsistent with a sense of dependence upon and gratitude to the Lord Jesus Christ (vv. 1–3). It is also contradictory to the mission of Christ, for He came to unite all nations in the praise of God for His faithfulness and mercy. Why is selfishness so divisive to the church and so destructive to its calling?

2. Emotion is part of Christian experience (v. 13). Feeling does not determine truth, but it is involved in a right reaction to truth. The Christian has distinctive sorrows over sin (2 Cor. 7:9–10) and joys in God (Rom. 5:11) that come from believing. How can Christians cultivate a biblical emotional life? What role does the Holy Spirit play?

3. Paul's heart beat to bring the gospel to those who had never heard the name of Jesus. Though a remarkably gifted theologian and preacher, his calling did not allow him to settle in to a stable school or church but propelled him outward to the nations. Not everyone has such a calling, but the church as a whole still has a responsibility to preach the gospel to all creation. How do you pray for and support those called to bring the gospel?

Notes

1

2

3

4

5

6

7

Notes

8

9

10

11

12

13

14

15

16

Notes

17

18

19

20

21

22

23

Notes

24

25

26

27

STUDY QUESTIONS

1. Verses 1–2: What does Paul say about Phoebe (KJV, Phebe), and how should they treat her?

2. Verses 3–5: Who were Priscilla and Aquila, and why did the churches thank God for them (Acts 18:2, 18, 26; 1 Cor. 16:19; 2 Tim. 4:19)?

3. Verses 5–15: What positive things did Paul say about these other believers?

4. Verses 17–18: How should churches respond to divisive false teachers?

5. Verse 20: What does this promise mean (Gen. 3:15)?

6. Verses 25–27: What attributes of God are mentioned? How does the gospel glorify this God?

DEVOTIONAL REFLECTIONS

1. The closing chapter of Romans reminds us that the church does not consist only of the great leaders like Paul but of many people serving in their own unique capacities. We find a great example in Priscilla and Aquila (vv. 3–5), who are always found at full stretch for the cause of the gospel. How can we follow in their faith? If Paul had mentioned you in this chapter, how might he have described you?

2. Heretics are not to be trifled with (vv. 17–19). Christian love does not condone letting the wolves loose among the flock. "Avoid them" (v. 17). If more Christians did this, there would be greater unity among those who do love the Lord and His truth. Why is heresy so destructive?

3. The gospel begins in the mind of God and is revealed to men, not deduced by them. It is God who sends it freely to sinners, whose accountability it is to receive it. If we have been privileged to hear this joyful sound and Spirit-enabled to believe in Christ, we are blessed indeed. God's glorious attributes, such as His eternity and wisdom (vv. 26–27), shine through in the gospel. Take some time to praise God for the glorious gospel of Christ revealed in this great epistle.